D1708841

INVESTIGATING THE UNEXPLAINED

# ALIEN ABDUCTIONS

By Lisa Owings

BLASTOFF!
DISCOVERY

BELLWETHER MEDIA • MINNEAPOLIS, MN

**Blastoff! Discovery** launches
a new mission: reading to learn.
Filled with facts and features, each
book offers you an exciting new
world to explore!

This edition first published in 2019 by Bellwether Media, Inc.

No part of this publication may be reproduced in whole or in
part without written permission of the publisher.
For information regarding permission, write to
Bellwether Media, Inc., Attention: Permissions Department,
6012 Blue Circle Drive, Minnetonka, MN 55343.

Library of Congress Cataloging-in-Publication Data

Names: Owings, Lisa, author.
Title: Alien Abductions / by Lisa Owings.
Description: Minneapolis, MN : Bellwether Media, Inc., 2019.
    Series: Blastoff! Discovery: Investigating the Unexplained |
    Includes bibliographical references and index.
Identifiers: LCCN 2018003678 (print) | LCCN 2018006178
    (ebook) | ISBN 9781681035925 (ebook) |
    ISBN 9781626178519 (hardcover : alk. paper)
Subjects: LCSH: Human-alien encounters–Juvenile literature. |
    Alien Abduction–Juvenile literature. | Unidentified flying
    objects–Sightings and encounters–Juvenile literature.
Classification: LCC BF2050 (ebook) | LCC BF2050 .O95 2019
    (print) | DDC 001.942–dc23

LC record available at https://lccn.loc.gov/2018003678

Editor: Paige Polinsky     Designer: Andrea Schneider

Printed in the United States of America, North Mankato, MN.

# TABLE OF CONTENTS

# A WAKING NIGHTMARE

Jay often wakes in the middle of the night. But this time, something is terribly wrong. He cannot move, and he can hardly breathe. Something is pinning him down. Dark figures gather at the corners of his vision. Are they shadows? Strangers? He tries to call out, to scream. Anything.

The figures look almost human. Almost. They stare down at Jay with huge black eyes. What do they want?

REC

5

The creatures are closer now, crouching over Jay. Then something touches him. Long fingers press into his flesh. He thinks he hears a voice. Is it in his head? "Jay. Jay."

## WANTING TO BELIEVE

Around half of all people believe aliens exist. Most of them also think aliens have visited Earth.

"Jay!" He jerks awake. "It's almost noon!" Jay never sleeps this late. He waves his mom away and grabs his phone before he can forget what happened. Online, he reads story after story about aliens. They are strikingly similar to his. Was he **abducted**?

# CLOSE ENCOUNTERS

Ever since humans first gazed at the night sky, we have wondered, are we alone? Scientists search deep space for signs of life. Movies and books imagine what might be out there.

Yet millions of people worldwide feel these questions are already answered. They say they have been abducted by aliens. Their stories are very similar. They wake suddenly or see strange lights at night. Aliens abduct and examine them. Afterward, chunks of time are missing from their memories. Could so many people be wrong?

# STAGES OF AN
# ABDUCTION

**1. CAPTURE:** Victims are taken at night, often from their beds or while driving. Many report seeing strange lights or UFOs.

**2. EXAMINATION:** Victims are studied by aliens, usually aboard a spaceship. Some abductees also speak to the aliens or get a tour of the ship.

**3. RETURN:** Aliens return victims, often to the same place they were taken. Many abductees report hours of "missing time" from their memories.

# MEMORIES OF ABDUCTION

In 1961, Betty and Barney Hill spotted a **UFO** along U.S. Route 33 in New Hampshire. It followed their car down the lonely stretch of highway before stopping directly above them. Barney saw dark figures at the UFO's windows. Suddenly, the couple found they could not remember the past two hours. When they returned home, they realized their car and clothes were damaged.

Betty and Barney Hill

## THE GRAYS

The Hills described one of the most
common types of aliens seen during
abductions. Grays are small and bony
with gray skin. They have huge bald
heads and large black eyes.

The Hills believed they had been abducted by aliens.
Psychiatrist Benjamin Simon used hypnosis to help
them recover their missing memories. The Hills described
their capture and examination in detail. Their story drew
national attention.

The Hills

# PROFILE: THE HILL INVESTIGATION

The Hills spotted the UFO on September 19, 1961. Two days later, Betty reported the sighting to an Air Force base. **Radar** confirmed a UFO in the area. The couple began working with Dr. Simon in 1963.

Simon hypnotized Betty and Barney separately. But both recalled being taken and examined by aliens. Betty remembered being shown a map of the aliens' home, which she later drew. Schoolteacher Marjorie Fish found it closely matched a star system called Zeta Reticuli. The Hills' story remains one of the most famous abduction cases.

# THE HILLS' U.S. ROUTE 33 TIMELINE

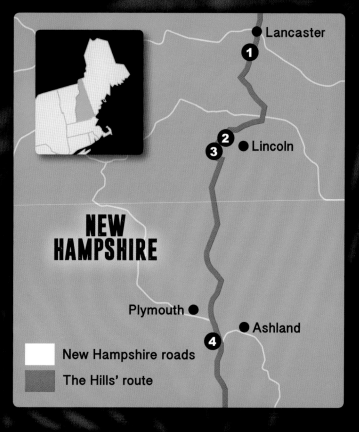

Lancaster

1

2
3 Lincoln

**NEW HAMPSHIRE**

Plymouth

4 Ashland

☐ New Hampshire roads
■ The Hills' route

**1: UFO first sighted**
**2: Barney sees dark figures**
**3-4: The Hills "lose time" for 32 miles**
**(51 kilometers)**

**hypnosis**

After the Hill case, abduction reports rose. Hypnosis became the main way to **investigate** alien abductions. Memories were seen as dependable **evidence**. The abductee's own brain might have blocked these memories. But they were still in there. A skilled hypnotist could reveal them.

REC

## THE STARCHILD SKULL

In 1930, a girl found a large skull some
believed was alien. DNA testing in 1999
suggested it was a boy's skull. Extra liquid
around his brain may have caused his head to
swell. But further testing could not prove
his father was human.

Some abductees claimed to be part alien or have
alien children. However, more proof was needed. In the
1980s, **DNA** testing became possible. Researchers could
test DNA from abductees and suspected alien bodies.
No alien DNA was ever found.

In the 1990s, hypnosis became less trusted. Many scientists believed it created false memories. A person might imagine something so strongly that they felt it had really happened. However, respected psychiatrists like John E. Mack still used this method.

Mack **interviewed** dozens of abductees. In 1994, he wrote a book claiming their experiences were real. But **psychologist** Susan Clancy wanted better data. She gave abductees **personality** tests. This helped determine how likely they were to create false memories. Clancy released her own book in 2005. It argued alien abductions had scientific explanations.

John E. Mack

Susan Clancy

# TRUTH HUNTERS

Abduction investigations focus on drawing out abductees' memories. Scientific tools help support or disprove their stories. Scientists agree hypnosis and memory can be unreliable. However, many feel hypnosis can be a useful tool when used carefully. Under hypnosis, patients enter a state between sleeping and waking. What their hypnotist says becomes their reality.

## GONE FISHING

In 1976, four men went fishing in Allagash, Maine. While standing around a big campfire, they saw a strange light. The next thing they knew, the fire had burned to ash. Under hypnosis, they all remembered details of an alien abduction. Three of them still believe it was real.

# INVESTIGATOR TOOLBOX

hypnosis

lie detectors

X-rays

DNA tests

spectroscope

To recover memories, a hypnotist asks patients to talk about their abductions. She might ask questions or have patients describe things. Whether true or imagined, these scenes feel real. Until hypnosis, most abductees only have faint memories of being abducted.

# HOW X-RAY MACHINES WORK

X-ray machine

particles

film

implant

X-ray

1. Machine beams particles at body

2. Particles pass through flesh and hit film

3. Implant blocks particles to create shadow on film

Many abductees believe they have alien implants. X-rays can detect them. X-ray machines beam energy particles through a body and onto film. The particles pass through soft flesh, but hard objects block them. These objects appear on the film. Abductees can then have them removed and examined.

**lie detector test**

Lie detector tests show an abductee's physical responses to their memories. Machines track their heart rate and breathing while they answer questions. The data shows whether they are lying. Several abductees have passed such tests. That means they believe in their stories, whether or not they are true.

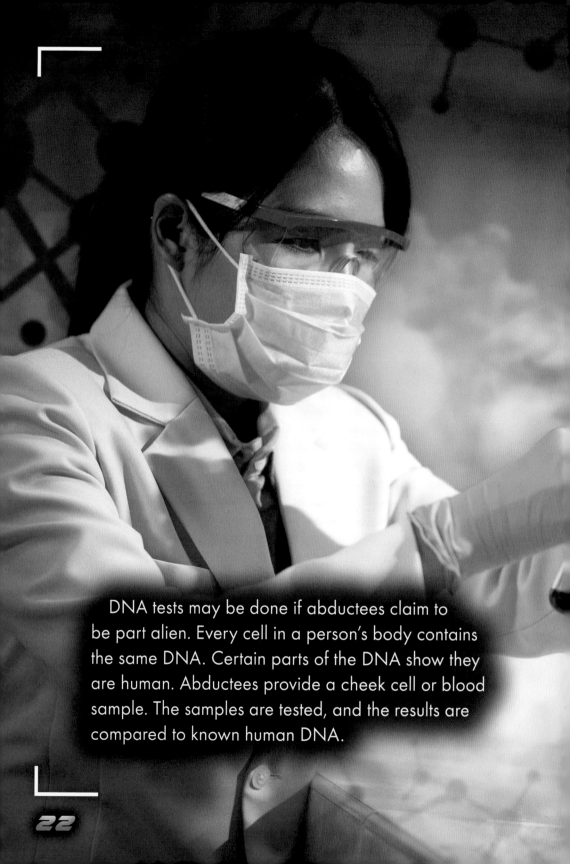

DNA tests may be done if abductees claim to be part alien. Every cell in a person's body contains the same DNA. Certain parts of the DNA show they are human. Abductees provide a cheek cell or blood sample. The samples are tested, and the results are compared to known human DNA.

## BETTY'S DRESS

After the Hill abduction, several labs tested a strange powder found on Betty's dress. They could not determine what it was.

**DNA testing**

Strange matter found after abductions can also be tested. Scientists use **spectroscopes** to study the substance's colors. They compare data with known substances to determine if it is earthly. They may do other tests based on the results, though the answers are not always clear.

# EARTHLY EXPLANATIONS

In general, abductees are not lying. And they do not have **mental illnesses**. Most are struggling to understand real memories they have. **Skeptics** study how people may come to believe they were abducted. Their strongest explanation is **sleep paralysis**.

## BUMPS IN THE NIGHT

Sleep paralysis may explain other frights throughout history. People around the world tell stories of ghosts or witches who visit at night. These monsters are said to sit on people's chests, holding them down.

sleep study

During deep sleep, our brains produce chemicals that keep us still so we do not get hurt. Some people wake up before these chemicals wear off. During sleep paralysis, people often see strange figures, hear voices, and feel fear. Someone unaware of sleep paralysis might think an alien abduction best explains their experience.

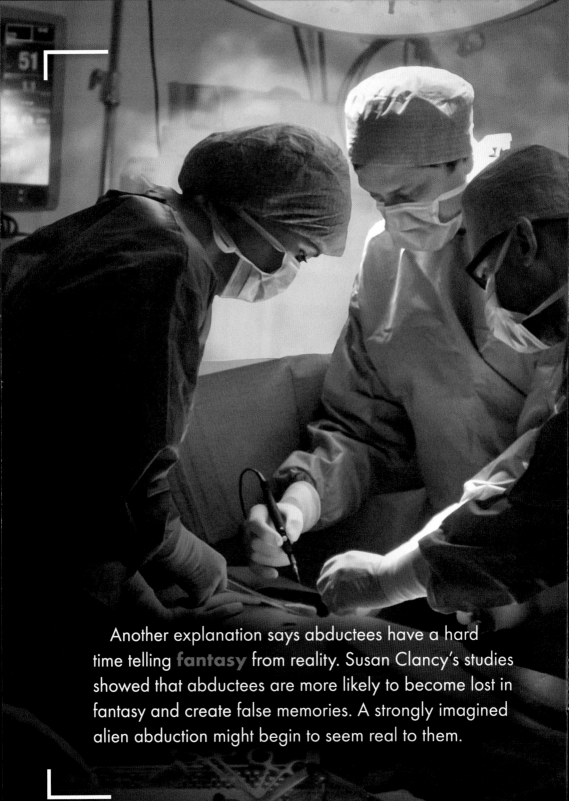

Another explanation says abductees have a hard time telling **fantasy** from reality. Susan Clancy's studies showed that abductees are more likely to become lost in fantasy and create false memories. A strongly imagined alien abduction might begin to seem real to them.

## FRIGHTENING FORCES

Some people's brains may react strongly to unseen forces, such as those that draw magnets together. This could cause them to see or feel things that are not there. More research must be done to know for sure.

Examinations are common in abduction stories. Scientists believe a small number of abductees woke up while having normal surgery. They might remember doctors' voices or the touch of metal on skin. Then they add details from movies, stories, and their imaginations.

# THE SEARCH CONTINUES

Are aliens really abducting Earthlings? Science says it does not seem likely. Evidence points to sleep paralysis as the most likely explanation. Still, no one has proven aliens are not among us.

Machines are constantly scanning the stars for signs of life. Billions of planets like ours exist, and some might support intelligent creatures. Could those creatures travel to Earth and snatch us up in the night? What do you think?

## SETI

SETI is a research center in California. Its name stands for the Search for Extraterrestrial Intelligence. SETI scientists search the skies for signals from advanced alien technology.

# GLOSSARY

**abducted**—taken against one's will

**DNA**—a tiny substance that carries information about the makeup of a living thing

**evidence**—information that helps prove or disprove something

**fantasy**—something imagined that is unlikely to happen in real life

**hypnosis**—a sleeplike state in which a person can still respond to questions and suggestions

**implants**—devices placed in the body; alien implants are thought to track humans, collect data about them, or control them.

**interviewed**—questioned or talked with someone in order to learn about them

**investigate**—to try to find out the facts about something in order to learn if or how it happened

**mental illnesses**—medical disorders that affect how a person thinks, behaves, or feels

**particles**—very small parts or amounts of something

**personality**—the way a person feels and acts that makes them different from other people

**psychiatrist**—a doctor who treats mental, emotional, or behavioral disorders

**psychologist**—a scientist who studies the way people think, feel, and act; psychologists may treat people through counseling.

**radar**—a device that uses radio waves to find and track objects

**skeptics**—people who doubt something is true

**sleep paralysis**—loss of the ability to move that occurs between sleeping and waking

**spectroscopes**—scientific tools used to split light into its separate colors; spectroscopes can help determine what a substance is made of.

**UFO**—an unidentified flying object; UFOs are often thought to be alien spacecraft, although any unknown flying object can be called a UFO.

# TO LEARN MORE

**AT THE LIBRARY**

Kenney, Karen Latchana. *Mysterious UFOs and Aliens.*
Minneapolis, Minn.: Lerner Publications, 2018.

McCollum, Sean. *Handbook of UFOs, Crop Circles, and Alien Encounters.* North Mankato, Minn.: Capstone Press, 2017.

Oachs, Emily Rose. *UFOs.* Minneapolis, Minn.: Bellwether Media, 2019.

**ON THE WEB**

Learning more about alien abductions is as easy as 1, 2, 3.

1. Go to www.factsurfer.com.

2. Enter "alien abductions" into the search box.

3. Click the "Surf" button and you will see a list of related web sites.

With factsurfer.com, finding more information is just a click away.

# INDEX

The images in this book are reproduced through the courtesy of: adike, front cover (alien);
Fer Gregory, front cover (boy), pp. 4-5; solarseven, front cover (UFO), pp. 8-9 (boy); Willyam
Bradberry, pp. 2-3; Science Picture Co/ Alamy, pp. 6-7; u3d, pp. 8-9; Chronicle/ Alamy, p. 10;
iStockphoto, pp. 10-11; Universal History Archive/ Getty, p. 12 (inset); Image Point Fr, pp. 14-15;
Gene Isenko, pp. 16-17; Harvard University Press Office, p. 17 (left); Steven Senne/ AP Images,
p. 17 (right); sdecoret, pp. 18-19; Andrey Burmakin, pp. 20-21; Wichudapa, pp. 22-23; Phanie/
Alamy, pp. 24-25; Gorodenkoff, pp. 26-27; Ursatii, pp. 28-29.